About the author:

Kathryn Rose

Kathryn is a social media strategist, trainer, author and speaker whose clients include major brands, international organizations, small businesses, and entrepreneurs.

In her twenty year sales and marketing career, Kathryn has become a specialist in increasing sales through collaborative strategies. As a Vice President of Sales at the Wall Street firm, Credit Suisse, she built a referral network that helped her increase sales to over $100m per year. She also created CT's first cable television cooperative marketing alliance, as well as the Arts Marketing cooperative, which helped these clients with limited marketing budgets achieve economies of scale.

She is a sought after speaker and trainer on using social media for maximum online visibility and using online marketing and social media tools to create referral networks and to increase sales. As an author, her books include: The Step by Step Guide to Facebook for Business, The Step by Step Guide to Twitter for Business, The Step by Guide to SEO/Video Marketing for Business and The Step by Step Guide to Linkedin for Business and The Parent's and Grandparent's Guides to Facebook.

Her speaking events include the Ladies Who Launch Global Conference, Real Estate University and Loan Officer Magazine. She has also spoken to school systems in Canada and the U.S. about online safety for children.

Connect with Kathryn on

Website: http://katroseconsulting.com

Facebook : http://facebook.com/katrose

Twitter: http://twitter.com/katkrose

Linkedin: http://linkedin.com/in/katkrose

Disclaimer: The Parent's Guide to Facebook: Tips and Strategies to Protect Your Children on the World's Largest Social Network is NOT associated with Facebook® Corporation in any way. International Copyright laws protect the material contained in this publication. You may not reproduce or resell the content in any manner. The information in this publication is for informational purposes only and in no way is this to be considered legal advice. Copyright KMH, LLC© 2010. All Rights Reserved

Foreward

Facebook is a phenomenon that cannot be ignored. And as Facebook has changed the way your teens manage their social connections, interactions and image it has also fundamentally changed the parenting landscape. This train has left the station, and you *must* be on board.

Changing social habits is not often easy, and many in our generation of "digital immigrants" find it challenging to embrace this new wave of social networking and internet-based communication. Your children are "digital natives," seemingly born understanding this digital world. If they are so natural at it you may wonder why you need to be involved. The answer is simple: *your children need your guidance*.

Just as you taught your child about manners, friendship, and values, you need to guide your teen about how to behave in the digital world. Your teen has a "digital footprint," as do you. This is something you'll want to manage and not leave to chance. If you don't, they may be learning the rules of the road from the road warriors themselves.

Some parents are intimidated and feel the learning curve is too high. Welcome to *The Parents Guide to Facebook*! Spend time as Kathryn Rose walks you through Facebook in a way that makes it easy and welcoming. You will wonder why you waited as you find a new world opening

up to you through this helpful and thorough guide.
The best way to truly understand Facebook is to use it yourself. Create your own profile, experiment with changing your status update, find your friends and relatives, and share photos within your network of friends. You are guaranteed to find some surprise connections and you'll begin to see the value of social networking and why it is important to your teenager. For me, it was when I saw photos of my niece's newborn son within hours of his birth that I truly appreciated power of this platform. The more you understand this tool the better guidance and support you are able to offer your teen.

Facebook is here to stay, and with *The Parent's Guide to Facebook* you'll find it easy to understand and embrace. Enjoy!
Sue Blaney

Sue Blaney is the author of
Please Stop the Rollercoaster! How Parents of Teenagers Can Smooth Out the Ride–
and co-founder of www.ParentingTeensInfo.com.

Join us at www.facebook.com/ParentingTeenagers

Introduction

Today we live in a world where technological advances seem to happen at the speed of light, with our children leading the charge.

This book is dedicated to all the parents who remember a world where:

- TV had only 3 channels and a dial that you had to get up and change
- we used typewriters for school papers and whiteout if we made mistakes
- the biggest advance in photography was the Polaroid picture
- we used the phone book to find telephone numbers
- the only way to send a message to someone was through the post office, with a stamp
- we were taught DOS in computer class
- Atari asteroids, pong and Super Mario Brothers were our video games

- **we needed a dime and a payphone to call our parents if we were going to be late on a Saturday night**
- **we called our iPod a "walkman"**
- **There was no internet and NO FACEBOOK**

With all of the emerging technologies in today's landscape, there certainly is the potential for confusion, distraction or misunderstanding. But, there are also new opportunities for communication and connectivity. For example, mobile phones enable us to quickly connect with our loved ones anywhere, anytime. No more need for dimes, or a dimly lit gas-station payphone. We can video conference with someone on a laptop from a coffee shop with wireless access half way across the globe or send email from an airplane, or exchange digital photos within seconds. The opportunities are endless.

As parents, we just need to make sure we understand the types of communication technologies our kids are using so that we can help ensure they use them as safely as possible. The more we know about these very public touch points available to our children, the more we can help them make the right decisions, have fun and stay safe.

Table of Contents

Preface: Sex, Drugs…Now Facebook? 10

Chapter 1: Signing Up for Facebook 14

Chapter 2: Finishing Up Your Profile 22

Chapter 3: Account Settings 30

    The Networks Tab: 34

Chapter 4: Privacy Settings Profile Information 38

    Bio or favorite quotation: 45

    Edit Photo Album Privacy 46

    Relationships: 46

    Photos and Videos I'm tagged in 49

    Facebook Places 51

Chapter 5: Privacy Settings - Contact Information 55

Chapter 6: Privacy Settings – Connecting On Facebook 57

    Facebook Internal Search 58

Friend Requests and Private Messages 59

Friends: 60

Chapter 7: Privacy Settings - Apps and Websites 62

The "Instant Personalization" setting 67

Public Search Listing: 70

Privacy settings and joining groups or fan or community pages: 72

Chapter 8: Privacy Settings – Block List and Bullying 74

Chapter 9: The Wall and News Feed 81

The News Feed 83

Chapter 10: Finding People on Facebook 85

Chapter 11: Creating Friend List 90

Chapter 12: Should I Accept A Friend Request? 96

Un-friending people: 101

Chapter 13: Removing Posts 103

Chapter 14: Reputation Monitoring 104

Chapter 15: HELP- My Ungrateful Child "Unfriended" Me! 108

Chapter 16: Creating a Facebook Group 112

Chapter 17: Uploading Photos and Videos 117

    Tagging Photos of People: 121

    Sharing Your Photos 124

    Un-tagging Yourself from Photos/Videos: 125

Chapter 18: Playing Games on Facebook 127

Final Words 130

Facebook Usage Contract 131

Preface: Sex, Drugs…Now Facebook?

Yes, it's true. Now there is ONE MORE thing we as parents have to have "the talk" about. Technology has brought many wonderful things into our lives. We have monitors that let us watch our babies while they sleep. We can TIVO our kid's favorite shows while they are studying. We are only a phone or a text message away at any time. However, with all the great things technology has offered us, it has also introduced some potential downsides as well.

I want to mention here that I LOVE Facebook. I began my journey to be a Certified Social Media Strategist to help business professionals learn how to engage and use social media platforms, such as Facebook, to enhance and build a client base and online reputation. In addition, I have used Facebook to connect to long lost friends, relatives and engage in conversations with other people outside my normal sphere of influence.

In my research on the business aspects of connecting, I

realized how many people, especially children, are not aware that their **personal** information is posted in cyber-space for all to see. It is for this reason I wrote the very first "Facebook Guide for Parents" and have since spent countless hours researching and updating to provide you with the most up to date book of Parent's Facebook tips and information.

I am a mom and an Aunt. I understand how important it is for parents and guardians to understand these new social networks and all their positive traits, while at the same time protecting ourselves and the young people in our lives from the potential harm they can cause. And I'm not just talking about on-line predators. I'm talking about their future reputations, college applications and even job interviews that can be affected inadvertently from a long forgotten post on Facebook.

I am not a child psychologist, doctor or teacher. But as a parent, and an aunt, and a social media professional, I have some experience talking to the kids in my life about safety online and I want to help you do the same. With the information provided here, I encourage you to engage in conversation with your children. I remember some of the downright stupid things I did in my youth and I am secretly glad this type of technology wasn't around to tempt me into making bad decisions worse by having them posted online for the world to see. Polaroid pictures were scary enough. Those pictures of bad hair, college parties and spring break probably would not have been a good thing to have floating around out there on the web then, or today. I have the gift of hindsight, and as parents, it's now our job to point our kids in the right direction online.

Consider these Facebook Statistics (most from Facebook others are sourced as noted):

- **Facebook has 600 million users**
- **If Facebook were a country, it would be the 3rd largest in the world**
- **Over 9 million U.S. children between the ages of 13 and 17 are registered Facebook users. (source** http://www.checkfacebook.com**)**

- **50% of our active users log on to Facebook in any given day**
- **Average user has 130 friends**
- **People spend over 500 billion minutes per month on Facebook**

Activity on Facebook
- **There are over 160 million objects that people interact with (pages, groups and events)**
- **Average user is connected to 60 pages, groups and events**
- **Average user creates 70 pieces of content each month**
- **More than 25 billion pieces of content (web links, news stories, blog posts, notes, photo albums, etc.) shared each month.**

Global Reach
- **More than 70 translations available on the site**
- **About 70% of Facebook users are outside the United States**

Chapter 1: Signing Up for Facebook

If you don't have a Facebook profile yet, please take the time to read this chapter and to set one up. Chances are your child does have a profile and the only way to find out is if 1) they tell you, 2) you "Google" or search the search engines for their name and their profile comes up or 3) if you have a Facebook profile and can find them yourself. Facebook is a gigantic playground and just as you'd want to get the lay of the land at any physical playground where your child spends time, it's important for you to understand this virtual playground. You'll want to educate your child about safety and you'll want to meet the other adults and children who hang out there.

If you know that your child has a profile, why not ask them to walk you through the set up? You can learn the steps here, but sitting with them makes them more involved in the process and they will take pride in teaching you something. They'll also know that you will now be on Facebook and even this knowledge could help them make better choices when posting comments and interacting with their friends. Telling them you are joining could open up an important dialogue and, once you've finished reviewing this book, you might even be able to teach them a thing or two!

So, let us get started with setting up a profile:

(even if you've already signed up you may benefit from some of this information, so don't be too quick to jump ahead)

Go to http://facebook.com,

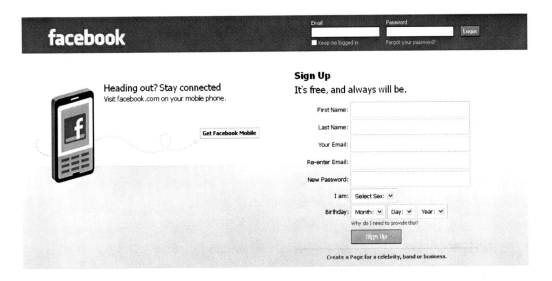

Go ahead and enter your information. Creating an account is free. I will show you, step-by-step, how to keep your profile as private as you would like.

Many people ask, "Why do I need to put in my birthday?" Facebook has a policy that no one under 13 years of age can have an account. That doesn't mean, however that your pre-teen hasn't gotten around this by putting in a fake birth date. Facebook works on the honor system and, as I've found out personally, some of children as young as eleven had active Facebook accounts.

Step 1: Find Friends

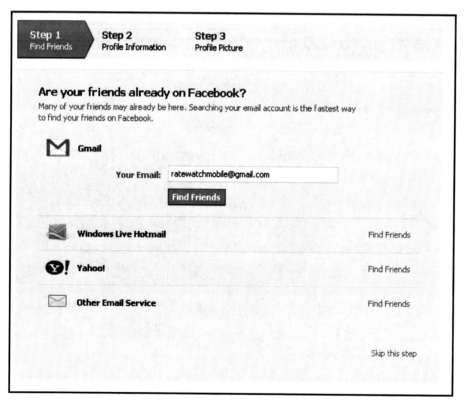

I never recommend you give up your email list—ever. But, if you would like to start connecting quickly with friends, go ahead and give your email address and password to

allow Facebook to access the email addresses of your friends to match them to their Facebook profiles. Otherwise, just click "skip this step." You can always go back and invite friends later.

Step 2: Profile Information

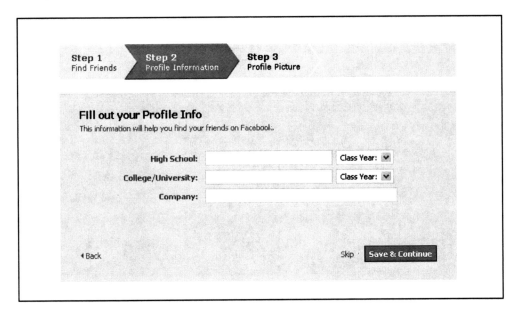

On this page, you will be asked about your school information. You are not required to complete this section. However, Facebook uses this information to suggest friends for you. It is up to you if you want to provide this information. Even if you provide the information here, you do not need to make it viewable to everyone. You can decide about that later when you establish your privacy settings. If you decide that you do not want to provide this information now, you can always add it later, so click "skip."

Step 3: Profile Picture

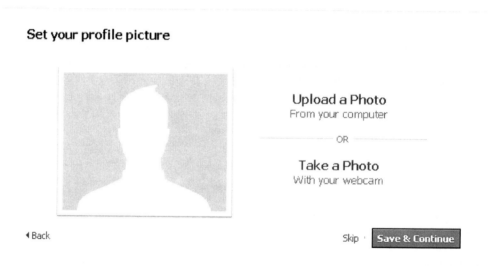

I encourage you upload a photo of yourself here. After all, it is called "face" book. If you have been using a digital camera and have been storing your photos on your computer or even on a photo-sharing site, this will be simple. Just click on "Upload a photo, then click "Browse" and select a photo of yourself from your computer. Click "upload." Note: This may be one of those tasks you can ask your child to help you with if this is the first time you are doing something like this. However, his or her idea of a "good" photo and yours might be quite different. (Skip the one of you with the crazy glasses.)

Once you finish Step 3, you will come to this screen:

Welcome to Facebook,

1. Search your email for friends already on Facebook

Your Email: [ ]

Find Friends

2. Upload a profile picture

Upload a Photo
From your computer

OR

Take a Photo
With your webcam

3. Fill out your profile information

Help your friends find you by filling out some basic profile information.

Edit Profile

4. Activate your mobile phone

- Receive texts with your friends' Status Updates and Messages instantly.
- Update your Status and Message friends using SMS.

Register for Facebook Text Messages

Already received a confirmation code?

5. Find people you know

Search by name or look for classmates and coworkers.

Enter a name or email

6. Control what information you share

Learn more about privacy on Facebook.

If you have already uploaded a picture, step 2 will not be visible. Before you do anything on this screen, let's move to step three and fill out your profile information.

Chapter 2: Finishing Up Your Profile

I recommend that you complete your profile set up and then move on to creating your privacy settings because there you'll see the types of information Facebook can capture. **Entering your information in these fields is completely voluntary.** You do not need to answer *any* of the questions in this section or fill out any information. You may include some, all or none of the information Facebook asks you to provide here.

If you just set up a profile click on Edit Profile here:

If you already have a profile, you will find the edit profile area under your name on the "home page."

Once you do that, you will be taken to this Basic Information screen:

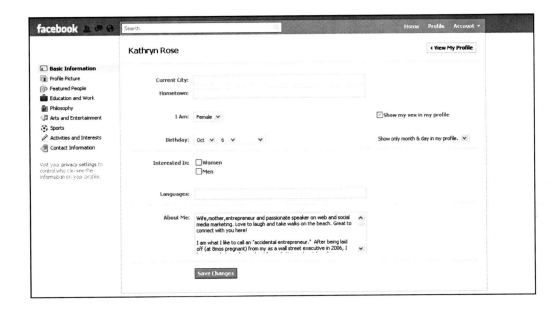

Here are the areas of information that you can fill in:

- **Basic Information**
- **Profile Picture**
- **Featured People**

- **Education and Work Information**
- **Philosophy**
- **Arts and Entertainment**
- **Sports**
- **Activities and Interests**
- **Contact Information**

Basic Information: This section collects your basic information and it is not necessary for you to answer all the questions.

It is recommended that you NEVER show your full birthday in your profile. This is the kind of information can lead to identity theft. Facebook's default setting is to "show my full birthday in my profile." To change this, click on the drop down arrow and change it to "show only month and day." If you don't want your birthday to show up at all, change it to "Don't show my birthday in my profile." Facebook is a social network, however, and wishing people a happy birthday is a wide spread practice, so you may want to consider showing at least your month and day.

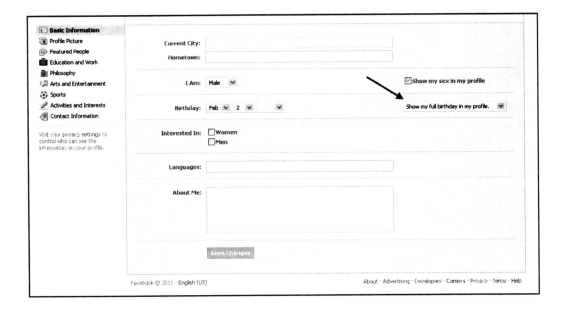

Current City and Hometown may very well be relevant if you are trying to connect to local people or to help people who may know you to find you.

However, the "interested in", may be something you want to keep private. Again, none of these fields are required. Fill them according to your comfort level.

I would recommend that you fill in the "about me" section with your bio.

Profile picture: This is self-explanatory. However, you will see a box at the bottom that says "row of photos at top of profile." Facebook shows the last 5 photos that you upload to your profile. We will get into photo sharing a little later.

Featured people:

```
Relationship Status:  Married        v  to

Family:                              Select Relation: v  x
                Add another family member

Featured Friends: Create new list

          Save Changes
```

In this area you can enter information such as your relationship status, add in your partner's name and link it to your partner's profile, and link to your children's and family members profiles. Again, none of this information is required; it is completely to your discretion. I do not recommend you add young family member's names to your profile especially those of younger children.

There is another area, called "Featured Friends". You can select specific groups of friends to be shown at all times on your Facebook profile. To create a featured list either go to the featured people area or go to the friends area on your profile and click on the "pencil" icon and it will bring you to the featured people screen.

Education and Work: The next screen to view and update is the Education & Work screen. Here's where you'll have the opportunity to add your High School, College and University details. Facebook also uses this information to suggest potential connections with other graduates from the same schools. This is a great way to connect with people from your past both socially and professionally. If you feel comfortable sharing your work information, go ahead and enter it as well.

Philosophy: On this screen you can choose to fill in your religious beliefs, political views, etc. Again, this is information is not required.

Arts and Entertainment, Sports and Activities and Interests: These sections allow you to fill out music, books, television shows, sports teams and topics you like, etc. This information can be used to suggest friends to you and Facebook uses it to target advertising.

Contact information: I recommend that you do not enter all of your personal information. However, if you have a business website and you'd like to use Facebook to attract potential business clients, it can't hurt to post it here. But you may not want to include your full address and phone numbers for everyone to see.

There have been some high profile news stories about people posting their vacation plans on Facebook and then being robbed. While this is a rare concern, you wouldn't post your vacation plans on your front lawn. That's what it's like to include your full address, phone number AND tell the world through Facebook that you're away for a month and your guard dog is in the Bow Wow boarding house. It sounds crazy that people would be so willing to share such private details about their lives but I see it all the time and want to warn you about the risks. Sharing details about your life is what makes social networking social but at times children forget or dismiss the possible dangers and share too many intimate details. It's necessary to remind our children that some details about their and their family's lives are private and should not be shared on Facebook or any other social networking website.

Now that you are done editing your profile, let's move on to Account Settings.

Chapter 3: Account Settings

In this chapter I'll review your Account Settings. This covers the overall configuration of your account, name, and user ID, as well as some additional things such as notifications and language.   You can access the Account settings from the drop down menu on the top blue navigation bar all the way to the right under "Account."

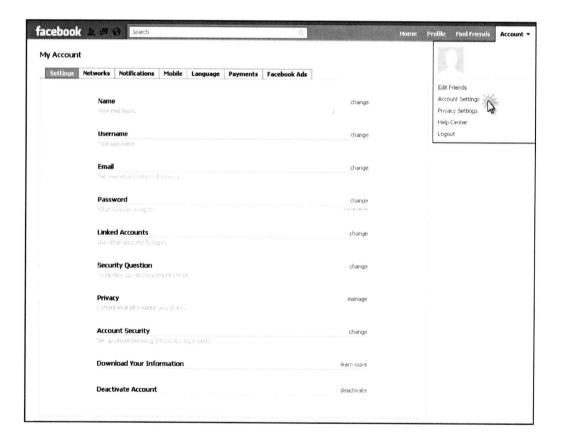

- On the **Settings tab** check to be sure all of your information is correct.

- Under "name"-- If you have a maiden name or another name you go by, you may want to add it here.

- Username: Facebook allows you to create a unique username for your profile which makes it easy to share with friends or to put on your business card. A personal url will look like this http://facebook.com/katrose (which is my username)

- Email: you can see what your contact email looks like. You will also have the option to adjust your privacy settings regarding contact information. I will cover privacy in detail later in this book.

- Password: change or update your password here.

- Linked accounts: You can link your account to your email accounts and other outside accounts but I suggest that you keep your Facebook account separate from other networks to keep tighter security levels on your passwords.

- Security question: if you ever have to contact Facebook, this will be the question they ask to identify you as the account owner.

- Privacy: You can access the privacy screens from here. However, as I mentioned, I will be covering privacy in detail in the next few chapters.

- Account Security: This is an important area. This area was made more robust after Mark Zuckerberg's (yes, the founder of Facebook) account was hacked.

These settings allow you to set a secure browsing option (which I highly recommend) and be notified if someone tries to access your account from a computer or mobile device that you have not used before. This way if someone is trying to "hijack" or "hack" your account, you will be notified. In this screen shot, this person only has email set up at this time. You can set up a mobile phone with Facebook and this feature will also ask if you want to be notified via text message. If you have a text-enabled phone I recommend that you set it up so you can be instantly notified.

Account Security
Set up secure browsing (https) and login alerts.

Secure Browsing (https)
☐ Browse Facebook on a secure connection (https) whenever possible

When a new computer or mobile device logs into this account:
☐ Send me an email

Save

Account Activity
View your recent account activity. If you notice an unfamiliar device or location, click "end activity"
Note: Locations and device types reflect our best guesses based on your ISP or wireless carrier.

What if you get a notification that someone has hacked your account? Go immediately and change your password.

- Download your information: Facebook added this option so you can download your photos and information if you wish.

- Deactivate account – this is self explanatory.

We will now move to the second tab: **The Networks Tab**

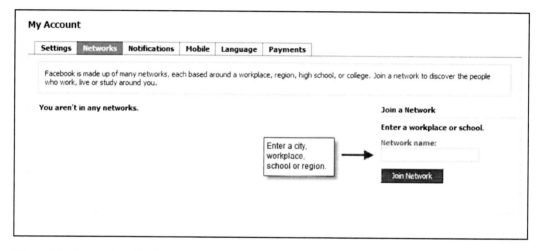

The Networks Tab:

The Networks tab will allow you to be added to a network of friends or classmates, if you would like. This will help friends, former classmates or business colleagues find you on Facebook.

I recommend you speak to younger children and teens about leaving this area blank. If strangers know the name of your child's school or the town you live in, it can become easier for someone to find your child off line.

The Notifications Tab: This feature allows you to turn on and off notifications for events, notices and other actions your friends take that are relevant to you. I find it beneficial to be notified right away with *some* of the actions, but annoying for others. Take time to explore your options and choose what is appropriate for you. You can always come back and adjust your settings as you become more familiar with how you use Facebook.

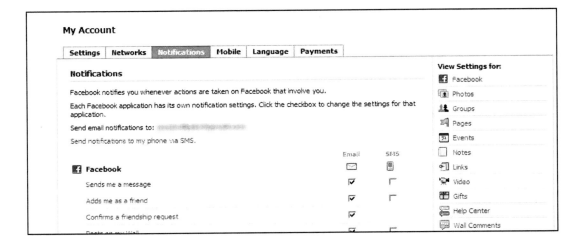

You can send your notifications to your cell phone via SMS but before you do it would be wise to be sure your wireless plan supports a text messages option.

Mobile Tab: This is a place where you can activate your smart phone (Blackberry, iPhone, or similar) so that you will be able to post your status updates, or upload photos and videos from your phone. You can also set-up your account to receive text message notifications for updates for different actions. For example: you can "subscribe" to a users profile via SMS or text messages and be sent a text message every time your child posts an update to their wall.

This may be a feature you would like to use to check in on your child.

Note that standard text messaging fees may apply depending on your mobile service plan.

Language Tab: Facebook is now available in more than 70 languages. You can choose your language preference from the drop down menu.

Payments: You can make some purchases via Facebook but most people set this up for purchasing Facebook advertising for their business. I recommend that you set this up only when and if you would like to purchase Facebook Social Ads to promote your business.

Facebook Ads Tab: Although Facebook says here they will not use your photos in ads, I recommend that you set this to "no one." Facebook could use your personal information for Facebook social ads "in the future."

Also, Facebook lets your friends know when you've "liked" an advertisement on Facebook. You may not want this information to be shared with all of your friends. To opt out, scroll down to the bottom and select "no one" as well.

Chapter 4: Privacy Settings Profile Information

The question I get the most when I am out speaking to organizations, schools and parents about Facebook is "what should I be aware of in order to protect my privacy and my child's privacy while using Facebook?"

Facebook offers a very detailed privacy platform and with the information outlined in these chapters, you can now go over both your settings and those of your children and set those controls to suit your comfort level.

As I mentioned, the "Privacy Settings" screen is accessible from both the "Account Settings" screen and the "Privacy Settings" areas.

To access the "Privacy Settings " screen go over to the upper right hand corner of your Facebook profile on the blue navigation bar and click on the "Account" tab and choose "Privacy Settings."

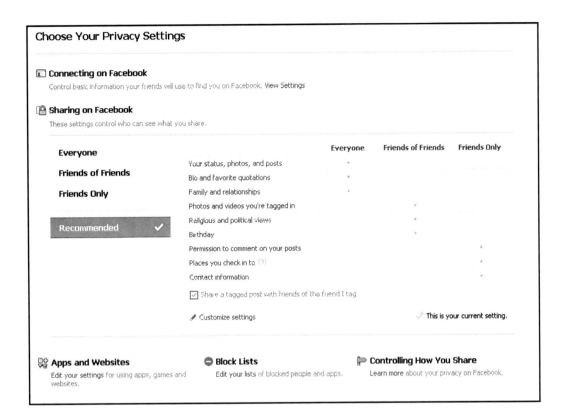

As you can see, Facebook's has a "recommended" default privacy setting configuration. Unfortunately, in some cases those settings are the *least* private. Here is a detailed explanation of the main 3 privacy settings.

1. **Everyone – This is not just everyone on Facebook, this is everyone on the INTERNET. This information is indexed by Google's search engine as well other search engines. Facebook says,** "the "Everyone"

2. setting works differently for minors (under 18) than it does for adults. When minors set information like photos or status updates to be visible to "Everyone," that information is actually only visible to their friends, friends of their friends, and people in any school or work networks they have joined. That's still a lot of people to view their personal photos and updates. I highly recommend that you check these settings and make sure they are not set to "everyone" for your child's profile. Most likely Facebook's own blocking system is protecting your child but why take a risk. IF your child were to fake his or her birth date (and this happens more than you would like to think) on Facebook, all of these things would become visible to everyone.

3. **Friends of Friends – This means all of the people you "friended" AND all of their friends.** Many people do not understand what this means so I want to be clear. Let's say you have not "friended" your boss but you have "friended" a co-worker who HAS "friended" your boss. If you have your settings

configured to 'friends of friends' your boss will be able to see that area of Facebook. If your "wall" settings are set to 'friends of friends' and you make a post about how much you hate your boss, he or she will be able to see it. Now might be a good time to remind you that what you post on Facebook should always be considered to be public, no matter what your privacy settings are set to. Use common sense and don't post things you wouldn't want others to see.

4. **Only Friends – The means that only people you "friend" can see your profile information.**

You also have the option to "Customize Settings"

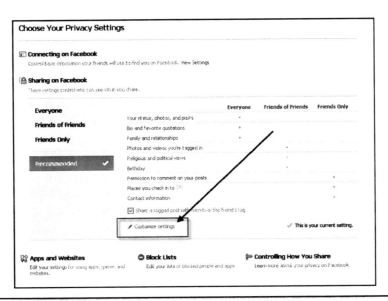

If you click customize, you will be taken to this screen that has these and other privacy choices:

If you click on the drop down box next to each of the choices you can "customize" further your exposure:

Once you click on "customize" on this screen you will see that the phrase "Hide this from" is a choice. Here, you can manually select friends that you would like to exclude.

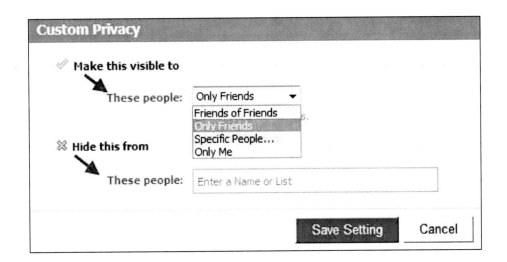

Using the "posts by me" setting as an example, customizing this setting might be useful if you post often about your child's soccer games and this information is not interesting to your co-workers. It might also be used to hide information about a surprise party from the guest of honor. But if you find you are regularly hiding posts from the same people because you don't want them to know what you are doing, then you might consider simply "unfriending" them. They won't be notified when you drop them from your friend list. The only way they can confirm that you have unfriended them is if they view your profile and the option to "Add as Friend" is available. In other words, if they can now friend you, they are no longer a friend.

Towards the bottom of this screen there is an option "Allow friends to post on my wall." Make sure that this is checked off to allow your friends to post on your wall and connect with you. If it's not checked they will not be able to leave you messages and your page will be a stagnant page with just your posts.

In addition, you can check how your Profile looks to other people by clicking on the Preview My Profile link in the upper right hand corner of the screen (see below).

This will show you how *most people* (in Facebook's words) will see your profile when they visit you. You'll be able to double check how you've set your profile and correct any oversights.

Remember, you can always come back to this same spot, make changes and adjust.

It is especially important for you to do this with your child. Double check his or her profile using the "preview my profile" button and talk to them about what they share with the world.

In many cases I recommended that you don't even fill out any of this information, i.e. interested in and looking for, family, relationships etc. but especially your children do not. There is no reason they need to tell people their all of this information but if you did you may want to go in here and customize your settings.

A couple of areas I want to draw your attention to:

Bio or favorite quotation:

This is where you can tell people about you, your business or your blog, and share your website information. This information can be updated or changed whenever you choose.

Edit Photo Album Privacy:

If you decide to upload photos, it is a good idea to set privacy levels for your photos on Facebook. In fact, you can set a different privacy level on each one of your photo albums, individually, once you upload your photos and create photo albums. This is a great feature because you will be able to share your "family" albums with your family, friend albums with your Facebook friends, and keep personal albums private from the view of your business Facebook friends, if you wish.

Relationships:

The likelihood is that your child will experience the ups and downs of teen relationships. It is also highly likely that they will "friend" someone they don't know well or that they don't know at all. Sometimes I see an example of a person changing their relationship to single, that status change goes out into the live feed and can be seen by others. Then they get messages from friends and friends

of friends, asking them for dates, etc.

Also, this public breaking up can cause some anger in the person who is the one being left behind. This can be a very sore point with teenagers and can lead to cyber bullying, hurt feelings, jealousy and other stressful situations your child doesn't need. I feel it is wise to advise your child not to advertise his or her relationship status.

I recommend that your child doesn't even say that they are in a relationship in the first place, but if they do this can ensure that no one sees that it has changed.

To make these notifications private, scroll down and set the Relationship area to "only me" By clicking on Customize and selecting "only me" in a pop up window. This means that only your child will be able to see their relationship status update change.

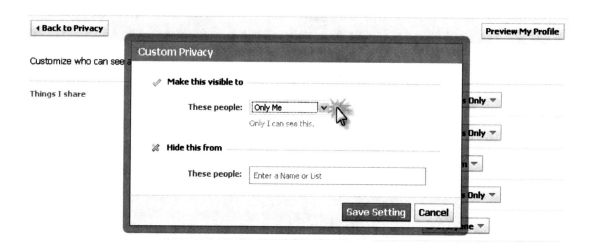

Photos and Videos I'm tagged in:

Things others share	Photos and videos I'm tagged in	Only Me
	Can comment on posts Includes status updates, friends' Wall posts, and photos	Friends Only
	Friends can post on my Wall	☑ Enable
	Can see Wall posts by friends	Friends Only

Think big hair and leg warmers…

"Tagging" is a way for your friends to identify you in a post or photo AND to notify you that they've posted something that might be of interest to you or that includes you, such as pictures.

I use my personal Facebook profile for business and have "friended" potential clients or parents of other children and I really don't think they want to see my college spring break pictures online.

This setting is even more important now with the changes to the Facebook's profile platform which happened in late 2010. The last 5 photos that you either upload yourself or that your friends upload and TAG you in, will by default, be visible on your profile.

Now you can't stop friends and relatives from posting unflattering, silly or embarrassing photos of you if they insist on doing so despite your protests, BUT IF the photo does get posted and you wish it didn't, you can certainly "untag" yourself so that at least the photo is not identified with your name and doesn't show up on your Facebook profile. To do this, find the picture you've been "tagged" in and beside your name, click on "remove tag" and this picture will no longer be linked to your profile on Facebook. Again, the photo will not be deleted from

Facebook, only from your profile. I will cover tagging in a chapter later in this book and go into more detail.

As displayed in this screenshot, people can see your photos by either clicking View Photos of "friend's name" or clicking on the "Photos" tab on your wall.

Here's an example of a photo tag gone wrong:

If you were Michael you might not want your current business colleagues or future college admissions officers to see this photo. (provided by the blog http://myparentsjoinedfacebook.com).

You can control this setting, much like the "Relationship" area, go to the "Photos and videos I'm tagged in." Then click "Customize" and make sure it is set to "only me." This way if a photo is uploaded and tagged the only person who sees it is the profile owner, either you or your child.

Get those photo privacy settings in place!

Facebook Places

In August 2010, Facebook introduced "Facebook Places" a way to share where you are in real time by "checking in" via an application on your smart phone, like an iphone or a blackberry. As of this writing, this feature is only available on the iphone but it won't be long before it is available for blackberry and android.

Basically, "places" uses the GPS in your smart phone to let friends know what you're doing and where you are. The premise is if one of your friends sees you are at a particular place, they can come by and hang out with you.

If you do not choose to check in, your location is not reported. In other words, it won't tell people where you are, unless YOU share it.

This can be a dangerous thing, letting people know you are away from home, an ex tracking you or your child down, can be a side effect of all of this sharing. You cannot disable places per se, just don't use it. But in terms of your child's privacy I recommend that you go in here and set the privacy for "places I check in to" to "only me" that way if your child does share their location, no one else sees it. It is defaulted to "only friends" but as I know, there are many children who accept friend requests from people they do not know.

Two other "places" settings to be aware of:

- **Include me in "People Here Now" after I check in**: If you or your child "checks in" to a place, Facebook will find other friends that are in the same place and let their friends know.

- **Friends can check me into places**: This setting allows friends to check you in. Imagine you called in sick to work and are really at the ball game. Your "friend" innocently checks you in and you're friends with your boss or other co-workers. Not a good thing. Click on "Friends can check me into places" then click on the "select one" and click disable.

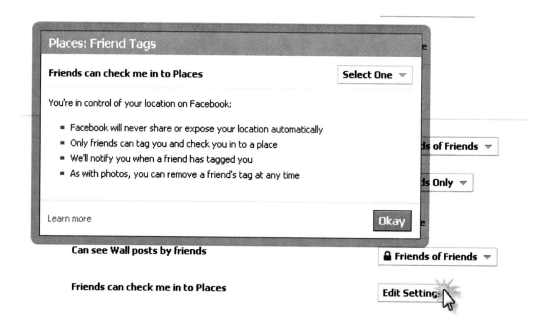

Even though Facebook says you can remove the tag if you want to, the damage may already be done. Safest bet, disable the feature.

The rest of the choices are self-explanatory and I recommend you explore these on your own until you're comfortable.

Chapter 5: Privacy Settings - Contact Information

On the Facebook Customize privacy screen, if you scroll to the bottom, you will find the "Contact information area."

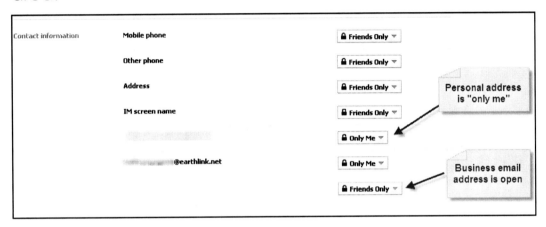

This area allows you to set the restrictions about who can who can see your contact information such as phone number, address, IM (Instant Message) Screen name (if applicable) and email address. Please remember the descriptions of what it means to share this information with "everyone," "friends of friends" or "only friends" and choose according to your comfort level. Again, you can change these at any time.

I do not recommend you make <u>any</u> personal information available for view to "Everyone." Also, again, unless you are using Facebook for business purposes, you probably don't want to even disclose this information in the first place.

One area I want to draw your attention to here is your email address. You may not mind if people you "friend" see your regular email address, but it might be a good idea for you to advise your children to set this to "only me" so that way, if your child does friend someone they don't know, that person cannot reach out to your child through their personal primary email address.

To protect your e-mail privacy and your child's e-mail address, click on the drop down box, click "customize" then "only me."

However, if you have a business, it may be a good idea to list your business contact information and make that available to "everyone" along with your web address as this information will be indexed by Google and other search engines.

Chapter 6: Privacy Settings – Connecting On Facebook

This area controls how you share some information. For instance, hometown, how people can find you on Facebook, and see what you "like" on and off Facebook.

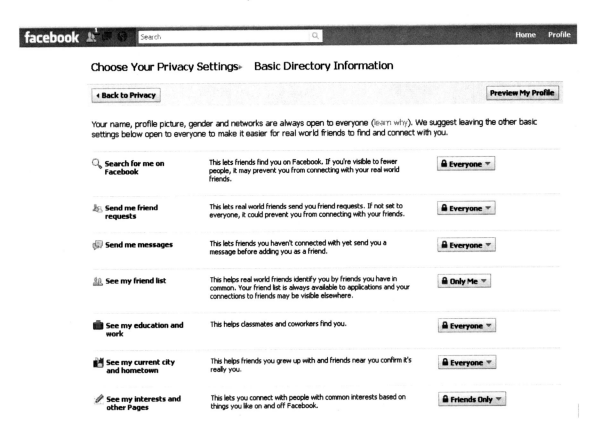

Facebook Internal Search

The first setting is "Search for me on Facebook". This automatically defaults to "Everyone" so you will have to go in here and decide by whom you would like to be found.

- ✓ Everyone
- ✓ Friends of Friends
- ✓ Only Friends

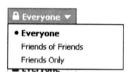

I recommend that you suggest to your child to set this to "Friends Only." This will completely remove them from the Facebook internal search engine so that the only people who can find them through search are those who ARE INVITED by them to be their friends. This means your child will have to invite people to be his or her friend on Facebook and not the other way around.

The reason for this is a simple one. It is easy for strangers to find young people on Facebook without even knowing them. For instance, if you type into the Facebook search bar a name like "Jane Smith," you will see a list of possible matches, with photos. If someone is interested in targeting young people, all they have to do is type in a name, look at the pictures and then send a "friend request" to your child. It's like looking through a yearbook in high school or a freshman face book in college (where do you think the name came from?).

Friend Requests and Private Messages

You may also wish to allow people to be able to "friend" you and send you a private message, however you may not want this option for your child, especially for younger teens.

| Send me friend requests | This lets real world friends send you friend requests. If not set to everyone, it could prevent you from connecting with your friends. | Everyone |
| Send me messages | This lets friends you haven't connected with yet send you a message before adding you as a friend. | Everyone |

If your child's profile is available for searches within Facebook once someone finds them, they can by default, either send them a friend request or send them a private message.

To turn off this ability for everyone to send your child a private message, find the area that says, "send me messages" and change it to "friends of friends" or better yet to "only friends."

Friends:

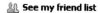 See my friend list — This helps real world friends identify you by friends you have in common. Your friend list is always available to applications and your connections to friends may be visible elsewhere. Only Me

Facebook defaults to showing your friend list to "everyone." This may be something you want to consider limiting for your child. When the world can see all of your child's friends, then you have limited control over information about your child on the internet. If your child's privacy settings are set tightly but his friend "Bobby" shows information to "everyone" and posts about going to Lincoln Junior High School's basketball game every Friday night, strangers who are motivated can put bits of information together by using a string of posts and "see" where your child is located in the real world and what their habits are. I don't mean to be alarmist, just realistic.

 To change who can view your friend list, click on the drop down menu to the right of "See My Friend List" and choose your own level of comfort, keeping in mind what it means to share with "everyone."

The other areas are pretty self explanatory but the last thing I want to draw your attention to is the "See my interests and other Pages".

This was added after Facebook gave the ability to add "like buttons" across the web. For instance, you could be on a news website and "like" an article. If you are logged in to your Facebook account, that information will be broadcast through your "newsfeed." This may or may not be something you want to restrict.

Chapter 7: Privacy Settings - Apps and Websites

In the Applications and Websites area under Privacy Settings, you can control what information is accessible to any applications you use, as they may publish stories in your Notifications and News Feed sections. As you make your profile settings more restrictive, less information is available to these applications.

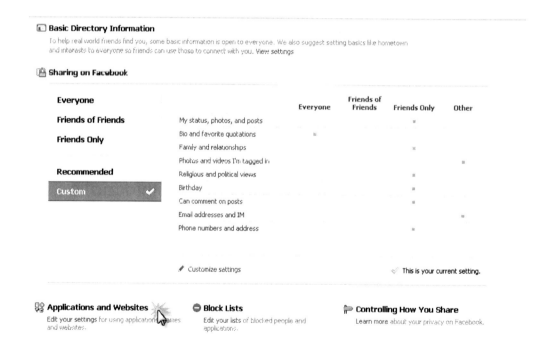

This area also houses your "public search setting" that is how people can find your profile in a "Google" or other search engine search.

Once you click on "Apps and Websites, you will come to this screen:

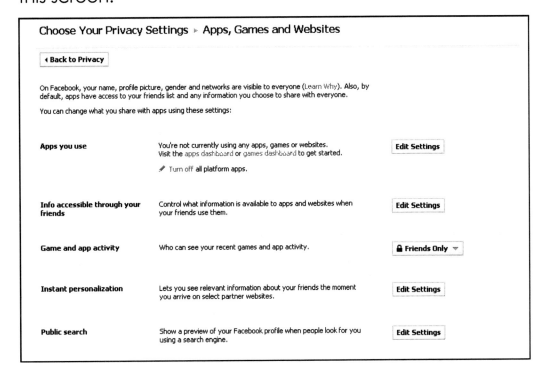

If you have been on Facebook previously, you may have a list of applications that you have used or have allowed access in the past. To remove them from your profile click "Remove unwanted or spammy applications."   Or you can "turn off all platform applications. "

To set restrictions on who can see your recent activity on games and applications, click on "Game and application activity." Here you can configure your settings as you like.

In the area that says "Info accessible through your friends," you will want to go through this and check the information that you want to allow your friends to share through the use of various applications on Facebook (like Birthday Calendar, or Greeting Card). Click on "edit settings" and you will come to a screen that allows you to control information that is shared.

The number of applications that are available can be overwhelming to say the least. Exercise caution every time you accept one. They often require permission from you to get all of your information as well as access to your friend's information, and while you are having fun, the application is using that permission to track a variety of things about you and access your information!

These applications are free because accepting one gives outside third parties permission to gather information about you and your friends that make up offline profiles that are then used as marketing data. Un-clicking your personal information will still give your friends access to the application, the application will simply no longer have access to your information. In my opinion, the trade off of your friend playing a game should not be accessibility to your personal information.

I suggest you un-check all these items to keep your information yours. If you have any of your information set to "everyone" it will automatically be checked off on this screen.

Some applications are fun like sending flowers and gifts, and others can be royal time wasters (for me things like Farmville, mob wars, medieval knights, little green patches etc.). You'll decide through experience which ones you enjoy, and you can always delete any applications that you decide later you do not want.

Some applications allow you to add information about yourself to your Wall and some will allow you to do special things. An application called Events will let you send an invitation to a specific activity to selected friends, and you might use this to set up a networking meeting or a party.

All of the games on Facebook are applications and if you find that you and your friends enjoy these, they are a nice way to interact with people. However, they can be annoying to others, so use at your own risk. If you find that you don't enjoy having people post news or requests for farm animals or Mafia connections on your page, you can block those applications so that friends can no longer send you requests to play those particular games.

And you can remove any applications you've downloaded if you decide later not to use them.

A very popular Facebook application is the Birthday Calendar application. This alerts you when any of the people on your friend list has a birthday coming up. You can then go to their page and wish them happy birthday. The application will automatically ask you if you want to give a birthday gift, but you don't need to do that. Just click the "x" in the upper right hand corner of that box, get rid of the gifts option and write your happy birthday note in the space provided. This is a nice way to remember friends and colleagues on their special day and is one of the most used applications on Facebook.

The "Instant Personalization" setting

In April, 2010, Facebook introduced "Open Graph" application which they call "Instant Personalization." In my understanding, this works much like amazon.com where once I log in to Amazon it shows me titles and products I may be interested in based upon past purchases. The idea is that users will want a personalized web experience so only content that matches their past likes will come up first.

What does this mean for you? Well, if you would like a more personalized experience than this will be great for you. The downside is this is an application and can collect personal information about you via the application or if your friends authorize the application it may collect information that way as well. For now, only 3 sites, Yelp.com, Pandora.com, and Docs.com have permission to do "instant personalization" in a beta test.

How do you turn off the personalization? You can go to the instant personalization setting and turn it off by unchecking the "allow" button. In my experience, this does not block the application from collecting information about you. You must go to the actual page and turn it off or say "no thanks". These three sites come up with a bar on the top saying "Hi Kathryn, Docs is using Facebook to personalize your experience. Learn More – No Thanks."

You can, however, decide what applications share about your personal information as I mentioned earlier by going to the "Info accessible through your friends" area and unchecking any information you do not want shared.

You can also prevent information from being shared by going back to all of the privacy settings and make sure that none of your settings are set to "everyone." Facebook says:

> **What you share when visiting applications and websites**
>
> Applications you use will access your Facebook information in order for them to work. For example, a review application uses your location in order to surface restaurant recommendations.
>
> When you visit a Facebook-enhanced application or website, **it may access any information you have made visible to Everyone** as well as your publicly available information. This includes your Name,

Profile Picture, Gender, Current City, Networks, Friend List, and Pages. The application will request your permission to access any additional information it needs.

What is the bottom line? Make sure your privacy settings are configured properly and do not share any information that you may not want accessed by applications. It is not necessary to divulge all of your personal information on Facebook.

Public Search Listing:

The last area I will focus on here is the "Public search" area.

This setting controls whether your Facebook profile comes up in a search engine listing like Google. In order to REMOVE yourself completely from Public Search Results (Google Indexing), simply click on the "edit settings" to the right of the "public search" area and un-check "Allow" under the phrase "Public Search Results".

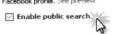

For children, Facebook states: "minors do not have public search listings created for them, so they do not appear in outside search engines until they have turned 18."

BUT I still recommend you check it for your child. Many children misrepresent their age on Facebook to appear older or to access things available only to adult users. While you may be vigilant about checking your child's profile, why take a risk.

You can see what your profile looks like in an internet search by clicking the "see preview" button, and again, I highly recommend checking out how your profile and your child's profile appear to the entire user base of the world wide web.

Facebook gets a huge amount of traffic from Google and the other search engines. Not all of your profile is displayed; only the information you allowed to be publicly shared when you set your privacy settings to "Everyone."

As you can imagine, this is an important feature to consider on your child's profile so that your child is not unintentionally showing all of his or her friends photos to everyone on the internet.

**Note: Potential employers or college admissions counselors have been known to do a "Google" search on prospective students or employees. Things posted on the internet live forever. In light of this, these settings are extremely important.

Privacy settings and joining groups or fan or community pages:

Joining groups, community pages and "liking" business fan pages are great ways to interact on Facebook. However, there are also privacy concerns here I want you to consider.

Even if your child's profile is private from people searching for them on Facebook, most groups and all fan pages are public.

If your child joins a group or "likes" a fan page that is public, they potentially open themselves up to being contacted by strangers.

For example, my niece told me about a person attempting to friend her by saying that they both play a popular game on Facebook. Since you only see your own Facebook friends while playing games, I went to investigate. It turns out she had joined a public group, and all a stranger in that group had to do was click on her picture to be able to send her a friend request. This is important for parents, and their children, to know. It bears repeating. Most groups, fan pages and community pages are public.

Chapter 8: Privacy Settings – Block List and Bullying

Unfortunately, our children, much like we were, are subject to the old saying, "kids can be so cruel." But online, the cruelest comments, videos and photos posted about them can haunt them forever. The impersonal quality of not being in the same room with each other can allow children to say and do things they might not say or do in person. They perceive an anonymity that does not exist and parental guidance in this area is a computer age challenge that needs to be addressed.

The first thing I recommend, of course, is that you really talk to your kids about the consequences of putting things online that are negative, downright mean or that don't present them in the best light. You want to be clear that you will not accept any behavior from your child that would be emotionally harmful to another child. In other words, you want to protect them from being bullied AND from becoming a bully. Both can be equally devastating to young lives.

If your child is being harassed, there are a couple of different things you can do, one is blocking users. Facebook gives you the option to actually block individual people from interacting with you. Of course, instead of "blocking" people, you can also always "unfriend" them. When you "unfriend" someone they do NOT get a notification about it. Only you will know that you "unfriended" them until they try to view your page. At that point they will realize they are no longer on your friend list. You can go to the privacy settings and click "block list." Add the person's name and they will be blocked--which ultimately means that your profile will no longer be visible to them when searching for you. Many people use this for ex-spouses and others they do not want to find them online.

You can also report a person who is bullying or harassing you or your child by clicking on "report this person" on their profile page.

The next thing I recommend is searching Facebook to look for potential Group or Page directed at your child.

Some kids are setting up groups and pages with titles such as "I Hate Jane Smith." These are hateful ways to hurt others and your child might be so upset they don't tell you about them. Additionally you'll want to make sure that your child does not participate in any of these "hate" pages about other children. Take a look at your child's INFO tab on their profile to verify that the Groups and Pages they participate in are appropriate.

Go to the search bar and type in your child's name. Click on the magnifying glass to bring up all results. Then make sure to highlight "pages" or "groups." This will bring up the list of pages or groups that could have your child's name in the title. **These pages and groups are against Facebook's terms of use and can be taken down so be sure to report them.**

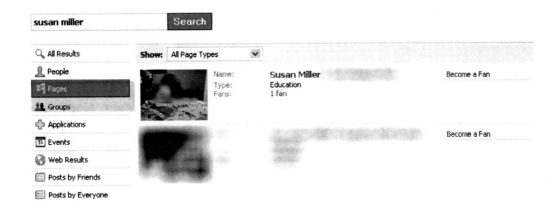

Here's how to report a page. Go to the offensive page and scroll to the bottom, then click report page Facebook will give you some choices about why you are reporting the page. Click the appropriate choice and then click "submit".

This is completely anonymous and your child doesn't even have to know you did it if you don't want them to.

Facebook also has some resources on the site to help you regarding child safety: Go to Account, then click on Safety and go to Help Center and follow the instructions.

There are also, some great resources available on the internet that specifically focus on cyber bullying and I recommend you take a look at these sites. http://cyberbullying.us http://bullypolice.org. Facebook is a founding member of the StopCyberbullying Coalition http://stopcyberbullying.org

Every once in a while I search for pages I think are cruel and report them. I just think that Facebook should be fun for everyone and not a pulpit for spreading hate messages.

You also need to speak to your child about not bullying OTHERS; children, teachers or anyone else. In one of my searches for offensive content while writing this book, I found a page that said "I Hate Mrs. 'Jones.'" Of course this is just as hurtful to an adult as it is to children. Many states are putting laws on the books to punish cyber bullies. School districts are getting strict about this as well.

There is a case in Massachusetts where two teens are being prosecuted for "identity theft" for cyber bullying because they don't have a statute on the books that clearly speaks to online content. There have been some extremely high profile cases recently of children using social media sites to harass one another with fatal consequences. Children can be arrested and tried as adults in the most egregious cases. State and national laws are catching up to cyber crimes. You don't want your child to break the law or harm another human being. Children don't always understand the long-term consequences of their actions and need your help in this area.

Facebook also has an area where you can offer suggestions on Privacy. Here is the link
http://facebook.com/privacyfeedback

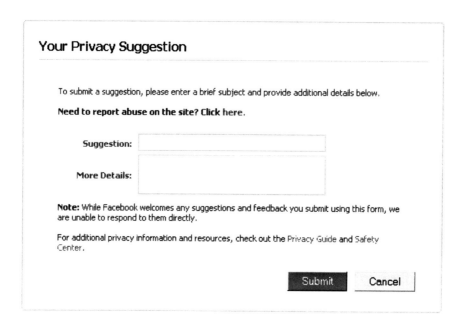

I have more information on how to keep tabs on your child's online activities in the "reputation monitoring" section of this book.

Chapter 9: The Wall and News Feed

You "Wall" is the space on your Profile page that allows friends to post messages, write notes to you and the space where you can write posts by simply creating a "status update."

Each message is stamped with the time and date the message was written. Your Wall is visible to your friends.

Things written on your wall by you or others are PUBLIC, unless of course you change the privacy settings so beware.

Here are some embarrassing examples of Facebook posts gone wild (provided by the blog http://myparentsjoinedfacebook.com):

> Michelle ▶ Chris : LISTEN TO ME...PULL UP YOUR BOOT STRAPS AND STOP LETTING ONE CLASS GET YOU SO STRESSED AND INSANE ABOUT IT...THIS IS LIFE ,SOME THINGS COME EASY AND SOME YOU HAVE TO WORK AT...THIS IS ONE OF THEM THINGS . YOU WILL NOT GIVE UP ! YOU WILL DO IT AND GET IT OVER WITH! IM HERE TO HELP YOU..NOW DONT LET ME SEE ANOTHER THING ABOUT SCHOOL SUCKING!
> 5 minutes ago Comment Like See Wall-to-Wall

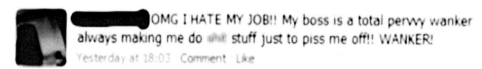

OMG I HATE MY JOB!! My boss is a total pervvy wanker always making me do shit stuff just to piss me off!! WANKER!
Yesterday at 18:03 Comment Like

Hi ███ i guess you forgot about adding me on here?
Firstly, don't flatter yourself. Secondly, you've worked here 5 months and didn't work out that i'm gay? I know i don't prance around the office like a queen, but it's not exactly a secret. Thirdly, that 'shit' stuff is called your 'job', you know, what i pay you to do. But the fact that you seem able to fuck-up the simplest of tasks might contribute to how you feel about it. And lastly, you also seem to have forgotten that you have 2 weeks left on your 6 month trial period. Don't bother coming in tomorrow. I'll pop your P45 in the post, and you can come in whenever you like to pick up any stuff you've left here. And yes, i'm serious.
Yesterday at 22:53

Below is an illustration of how "viral" a wall post can be:

"I write on Susan's Wall – it shows up in her "news feed" as well as mine. Even if my privacy settings are set to allow only MY friends to see my wall, Susans's may be set so that her friends, friends of friends AND their networks can see HER wall. Now my post is not private. It may be private for me, but not for Susan."

Bottom line: if you're not sure who is going to see a post on your wall, don't post anything private. The ONLY way to ensure someone is getting a private message is to click on "Send a Message" on the upper right side of a person's profile page.

The News Feed

Different users wall posts show up in the user's News Feed. Your News Feed (visible if you click on the "Home" link at the top of your page in the blue bar) is a collection of your friend's posts. The News Feed is Facebook's listing of posts by your friends. There are two options for viewing posts in your News Feed:

1. **Top News** is selected by Facebook and shows the posts from your friends that Facebook thinks are most interesting to you based on your recent activity and interaction.
2. **Most Recent** is an actual real time chronological listing of your friends latest posts presented in the

"live" stream of updates. If you have established friend lists, click on the arrow next to "most recent" and then you can sort posts by friend lists.

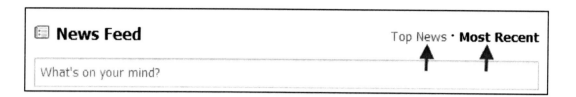

You can toggle back and forth to show the Top News or Most Recent.

Many users leave short messages and notes on their friend's walls to stay in touch. You can attach links to websites they might be interested or post photos they might enjoy. This is how you can keep in contact with your friends and stay current on their lives. You can post replies to their status updates to engage in conversation. Again, don't post anything that you want to be private.

Chapter 10: Finding People on Facebook

Whew, the privacy and profile settings are done-- fun, wasn't it? Not really I know, but necessary as you have no doubt discovered yourself.

While being a little scary for newcomers, Facebook is a great resource to reconnect with old friends, reach out to new ones and start connecting with people. In my daily life I wish I could be more connected. But with work, kids, pets, laundry, etc., it gets hard. Facebook provides me with a way to keep connected but only as much as I would like.

How do I find people? Start by finding people you know. Look up a long lost friend.

Simply type their name into the search bar and click the looking magnifying glass symbol on the right.

Once you have done this you will see some results :

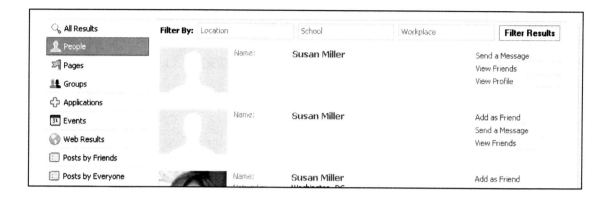

If the person has a common name like "Susan Miller," there can be a large number of results. So you'll want to filter by location, school or workplace and click "filter results."

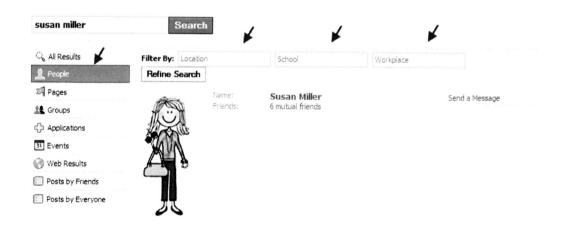

Once you start "friending" people, Facebook will start to recommend friends for you, based on your networks or friends you may have in common with other friends.

If you recently joined Facebook, another way to find friends is to go to the top right of the navigation bar and click on "Find friends."

If you have been on Facebook for a while and have a good number of friends, this option will not be shown. You can find friends either from the "people you may know" area on the right of the page, or the "find friends" area on the left:

Click on "Find Your Friends" and you will come to a screen that allows you to upload your email contact list (not recommended)and Facebook suggests friends for you and allows you to search for people.

If you would like to find former classmates, click on "show more", then "other tools." From here you can can search by your school name and class year and also find people you work with or used to work with. It's a great tool for reconnecting with people!

Search for your child's profile even if you and your child are not friends (yet). You can use the information below to evaluate their profile:

- ✓ Is their profile public? By this I mean, if you click on your child's name, it should say "Suzie only shares certain information with everyone. If you know Suzie, add her as a friend on Facebook."
- ✓ Can you see some of their friends? You may or may not think it is appropriate for outsiders to see who is on your child's friend list, especially because a user can click on the friend's name and then go to their profile.

What other information comes up? Does their school name or city? You can decide what you think is best for your child and help them adjust their privacy settings accordingly.

I have seen cases of a friend's child who is only 14, listed his high school on his public searchable profile so if someone is searching and finds him, they know where he attends school. Another example is a friend who found that her 12 year-old nephew listed his complete home phone number and middle school! Even though he isn't allowed by Facebook to have a profile, he had misrepresented his birth date in order to be on Facebook. It happens all the time.

Chapter 11: Creating Friend List

Facebook offers a great way to organize your friends into various groups. For example, you can create a list that contains your family members, another list for your friends from a book club, a list that has business contacts, yet another one that has all your friends from a particular networking group. The added advantage of creating lists is that each list can be assigned different privacy setting. Remember that a friend's privacy setting will always default to the most restrictive list you add them to.

A couple of notes about friend lists:

- ✓ You can place any friend into multiple Friend Lists.
- ✓ You can have unlimited number of Friend Lists.
- ✓ Each Friend List can have a different privacy setting.

Creating Friend Lists:

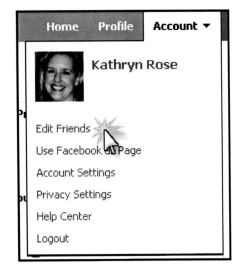
Go to "Account," click on "Edit Friends". This will bring up the listing of all your current Facebook friends.

You will be able to create a new Friend List by clicking on the "Create List" link.

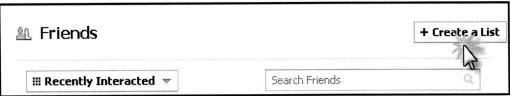

When you click on the "Create New List" link, a window will pop up asking you to name your list. Give your new list a descriptive name to help you identify it later. The search box in the upper right allows you to search through your friends to find the people you want to add o the new list.

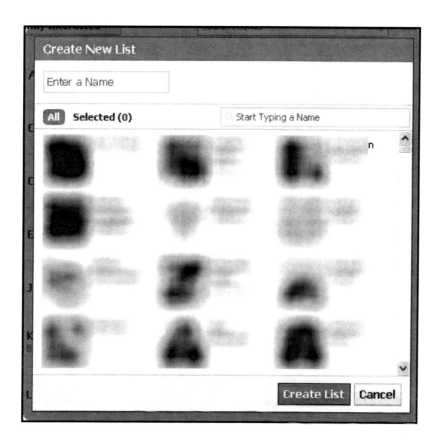

Clicking on a friend's name or picture will add them to the list, and their entry will now have a blue box with a checkmark around it to indicate that they have been selected as members of this list.

When you've selected all the friends for your list, click the Create List button to complete the process. This List is now added to your "Lists."

For example, I have a list named "Key Contacts" so when I go to my friends area I can click on "Key Contacts," only friends on that list will be shown.

Using Friend Lists:

You can create as many friend lists as you wish.

Facebook offers you to sort your "news feed" to either Top News or "Most recent". Once a list is selected, you will only see the updates from the people in that list in the in the newsfeed area.

For example, you could create a list for co-workers, family, close friends, associates from a club or organization and so on — and any time you wanted to check in with that group, you could do so very easily from your Home page without having to sort through lots of other posts.

The other way to use the lists is in setting your profile privacy settings. Remember the "customize" option when setting up your privacy settings?

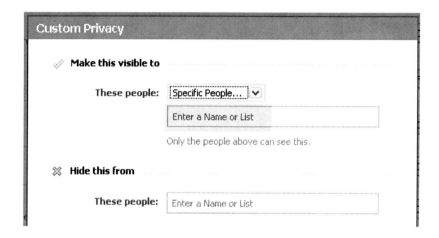

You can see here that "specific people" allows you to enter a "name or a LIST"

You can even use friend lists when you do status updates. On the "what's on your mind" area, there is a little "lock."

From here you click "customize" and then "specific people" and send your status update to only the folks on that list.

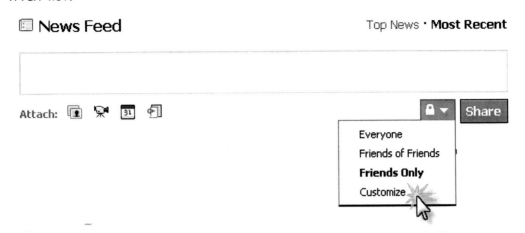

Chapter 12: Should I Accept A Friend Request?

So many kids think that they have to amass hundreds, even thousands of friends to be popular on Facebook which in their mind transcends to popularity in real life. Hey, I'm sure my friends and I would have thought the same thing at their age. But online you have to protect your information. As you saw in the privacy settings, if you're not careful about who you "friend," you could be giving away a whole lot of information you wouldn't normally give out in person. Let's face it. Would you give a stranger your address, phone number, vacation schedule or pictures of you or your kids? I think not.

You might not suspect that someone who doesn't know you or your child at all would even want to friend them, but it happens all the time. I get friend requests from total strangers every day.

You may want to "friend" a parent of another child in your son/daughters group just to connect. When I was growing up, all the moms in the neighborhood kept an eye on me and my friends when we were outside. Now we all need to do the same thing for one another's children when they're outside in cyberspace.

Friending people:

When you receive a friend request from someone you don't know, the first thing you should look for is a personal note. It is very important if someone is requesting to be your friend that they tell you who they are and why they are asking to be your friend. It's not enough that they say, Suzie Miller suggested we become friends because as you saw before, they could have gotten Suzie's name from a simple Facebook search.

Then EVEN IF YOU KNOW THEM, take a look at their profile. Is it public? How do you know them? Children should never accept a friend request from someone they do not know.

Even as an adult, be aware that many of your friends may be using Facebook for business and accepting friend requests from total strangers. So, as I mentioned, it's not a good idea to use just "friends in common" as your sole reason for accepting a friend request. Do your homework just as you would before inviting someone into your home.

From there you have two choices; either accept the friend request or click "not now."

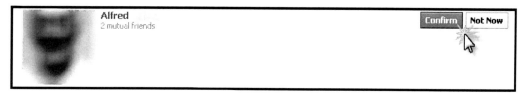

If you click "not now" This puts the person's friend request in to an area called "Hidden Requests." Don't worry; the person doesn't get a notification telling them you put them there. You can confirm the person later if you wish, and in the meantime if they go to your profile, they will just see that they are "awaiting friend confirmation".

Once you click "not now" another screen appears, letting you know that the request has been put into your "requests page" or you can choose the option "I don't know this person."

If you indicate that you don't know the person, this will block them from trying to friend you in the future.

This is very important to note because, once again, it goes back to privacy issues. If you or your child's wall privacy is set to "friends of friends" or "everyone", if someone sends you a friend request and you click "not now" that person still may be able to see your or your child's posts in their news feed. Be cautious when using the "not now" option, and always double check your privacy settings.

If you decide for some reason to accept a friend request later you can find them in the "hidden requests" area. To go to the "hidden requests area" go to the friend request link from your news feed on the right, click and scroll to the bottom of your friend requests, there you will see a "1 hidden request" link.

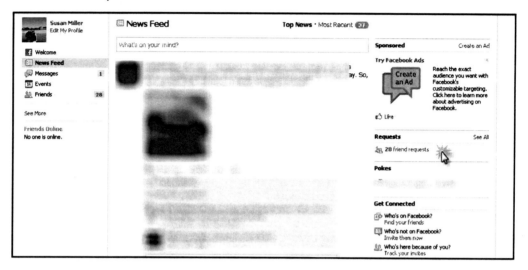

In addition to going to the bottom of the list of Friend Requests on the Requests page you can go directly to http://www.facebook.com/reqs.php to see the list of Friend requests.

You can also report the person if you feel it was an inappropriate request or a fake profile. I received a friend request from "Tom Cruise" and although I would be happy to be his friend, it is undoubtedly a fake profile. To file a report, click on the person's name, go to their page, scroll to the bottom and click "Report/block" this person.

If you choose to accept someone as a friend, check out their profile and their wall and make sure their content is appropriate. I always check my friends profiles to see if they put their birth date or give away other information I think should remain private, and if I see it, I then send a private message (**note: not a Wall post**) to the person letting them know that they should think about changing some of their privacy settings for safety reasons.

Un-friending people:

If someone you "friended" turns out to post inappropriate things or just posts sales message after sales message to attempt to entice you to buy something, you can easily "unfriend" them.

Go to the blue navigation bar across the top and click "Edit Friends."

In the left menu bar section click on either "All Connections" or below in the "Lists" section "Friends." This will pull up all your friends where you can make a choice on "unfriending" them by clicking on the "X" to the right

"Remove Connection" and confirm it.

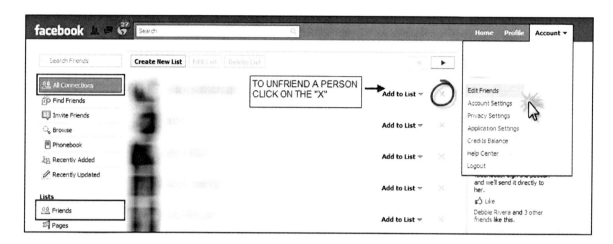

Don't worry. The person will not be notified. But, if they go to their own friend list or try and click on your profile, they will notice that you are either missing or they cannot access your profile.

Chapter 13: Removing Posts

OOPS! I messed up and posted something on my wall that I didn't mean to put there. Can I remove it? Yes!

How to remove posts once they are live:

Simply go to your wall, hover your mouse below the "Options" button on the upper right corner of the post and a "Remove" button will appear. Click on the "X" next to the post. A box will come up asking if you're sure you want to delete. You can delete your posts, as well as others who may have posted on your wall.

This removes the post from your wall and any of your friends' news feeds where it might have been posted.

Chapter 14: Reputation Monitoring

As a parent I understand how important it is to protect my child (and my own) reputation online. Once something is out there, it's out there forever. So how do you find it once it's posted?

FREE SITES

Google Alerts is a great free tool that emails you automatically when there are new Google results for your search terms. You can set up a Google alert for your name, your child's name or any subject where you want regular alerts. Google currently offers alerts with results from News, Web, Blogs, Video and Groups.

According to the Google Alerts website, you can sign up for 6 variations of alerts: 'News," "Web," "Blogs," "Comprehensive," "Video" and "Groups."

News alert - an email aggregate of the latest news articles that contain the search terms of your choice and appear in the top ten results of your Google News search.

Web alert - an email aggregate of the latest web pages that contain the search terms of your choice and appear in the top twenty results of your Google Web search.

Blogs alert - an email aggregate of the latest blog posts that contain the search terms of your choice and appear in the top ten results of your Google Blog search.

Comprehensive alert - an aggregate of the latest results from multiple sources (News, Web and Blogs) into a single email to provide maximum coverage on the topic of your choice.

Video alert - an email aggregate of the latest videos that contain the search terms of your choice and appear in the top ten results of your Google Video search.

Groups alert - an email aggregate of new posts that contain the search terms of your choice and appear in the top fifty results of your Google Groups search.

I recommend when you set up alerts, you make sure to use all variations of your name and your child's name including nicknames. The best way to set up the alerts is in **quotes**. For example "Your Name" this way you will get only alerts that include both of the words YOUR and NAME as one phrase. Otherwise, you could end up receiving alerts on any time someone mentions YOUR or NAME. In Susan Miller's case, she'd get notified every time someone mentioned the name Susan or the name Miller. That could be overwhelming and not useful.

How to set up Google Alerts:

Go to http://www.google.com/alerts

You can set this up so alerts are sent to your own email or set it up through a GMAIL account. You can set up multiple alerts for the same name across different categories if you like.

PAID SITES

There are many sites on the internet now to help you monitor your reputation. "Reputation Defender" is one of the sites I have found that does this for a fee and is much more in depth than Google Alerts.
Find it at http://www.reputationdefender.com

Search Facebook

You can also search Facebook to see if someone is referencing your child. To do this go to the search bar, type your child's name in, in quotes. Hit enter then when the page comes up make sure you go to the bottom and click "posts by everyone." This will bring up a search in real time of people talking about anyone with your child's name.

Chapter 15: HELP- My Ungrateful Child "Unfriended" Me!

This is every parent's nightmare! The simple fact is there is no way to force your child to "friend" you. Think of it as the diary of our day. Did you show your parents your diary?

For younger kids, it is probably a good idea for parents to exercise control over the accounts while giving kids enough freedom to learn appropriate online etiquette and safety measures. Many people recommend parents set up the account for the child and hold onto the password so the child can't access Facebook without your knowledge. I always tell parents to do what is right for you and your child.

I can, however, offer some tips on what you can do or not do to up your chances of staying on your child's "friend" list (all examples from http://myparentsjoinedfacebook.com):

Don't write embarrassing things on your CHILD's wall.

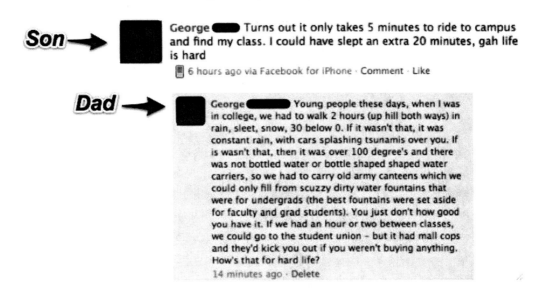

Don't write embarrassing things on YOUR wall that could end up in your child's news feed and most likely on to their friends' news feeds.

Don't freak out over every little post: pick your battles.

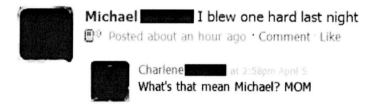

Don't panic if they "unfriend" you. Try and find out why they did it. Then, sit down and discuss the privacy settings with them. If YOU can't see what is going on, they should make sure NO ONE else outside of their friends can see either. Use this as an opportunity to start a discussion. Often your child will "friend" you again after a good discussion about boundaries and communication. This is a potential teaching moment and worth the discomfort.

If your younger child won't friend you, at the very least I suggest you insist on seeing their "Info" page occasionally to make sure they haven't exposed too much personal information. It is VERY likely that your child will friend someone they don't know very well, if at all. At least this way that person won't have access to your home address and phone number.

Each kid is unique; you know what kind of communication works with your child so do what is right for you.

Chapter 16: Creating a Facebook Group

In early October 2010, Facebook introduced a new group feature. Similar to friend "lists" (I covered that in a previous chapter and Facebook says that at this point friend lists are staying which is why I left them in this book), this new Facebook "group" feature allows you to group just some close friends, business associates, employees or whomever you would like and communicate just with that group. This is a basic overview as this is a new feature and will most likely undergo some changes.

To create a Facebook Group, go to the "Groups" icon located in the left menu bar of your "Home" page.

From here, you can search for groups and also create a new group.

To create your own group, click on "Groups" and "+ Create a Group."

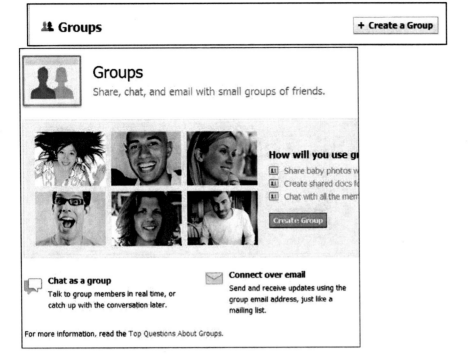

A box will pop up. Enter the name of your group and then the friends you want to add in your group.

Remember, you can add only your Facebook friends in the group you are creating. Type the names in the **Members** box (no need to type full name, after typing the initials, Facebook automatically displays your friend's name).

After typing all the names, choose the privacy level. You can choose is to closed group therefore all the members will be public (anyone on Facebook can see them) and the content will be private. Click on **Create** button. Add in a group name and then start typing in names of your friends to add to the group:

Your Facebook group is created. Just a reminder: be aware that the members of the group are PUBLIC but depending upon how you have the settings configured, the group content may be private.

The "groups" feature is opt-out meaning anyone can create a group with you in it, you will have to remove yourself if you no longer want to be in the group.

The interesting thing about the new "groups" is that you can chat as a group. The "chat" feature is an instant message type feature in facebook.

You will also at some point be able to share your status updates with just these folks in your group, again, similar to Facebook Friend lists.

To edit your group once it is set up click on the group title, then go to the right of the screen

And click edit group, you can change the name, the privacy settings and you can even set up a specific email for your group.

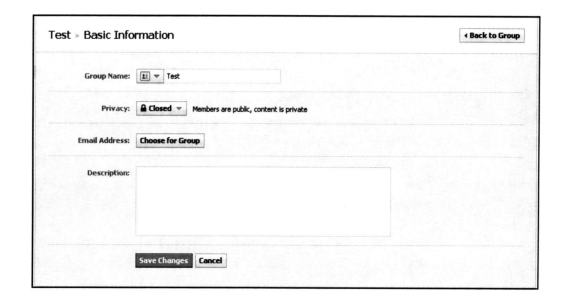

Chapter 17: Uploading Photos and Videos

One of the most popular applications on Facebook is the Photos application. The main features of this application are:

- Upload unlimited numbers of photos.
- Create photo albums.
- Post comments on your friends' photos and albums.
- Privacy settings for individual <u>albums</u>, limiting the groups of users that can see an album. For example, the privacy of an album can be set so that only the user's friends can see the album, while the privacy of another album can be set so that all Facebook users can see it.

According to Facebook there are:

- 1.7 billion user photos uploaded to their servers
- 2.2 billion friends tagged in user photos
- 60+ million photos added each week to Facebook servers

- 3+ billion photo images served to users every day
- 100,000+ images served per second during peak traffic windows

One of the most fun things you can do with Facebook is share photos and videos. There are a couple of different ways to upload photos and videos. The process is the same for both (photos AND videos).

You can find Photos by clicking on the "Photos" link in the left menu bar of the "profile " page. Click on upload photos to upload a new photo or album. Or in your own photo array, you will see that each photo is tagged by its name.

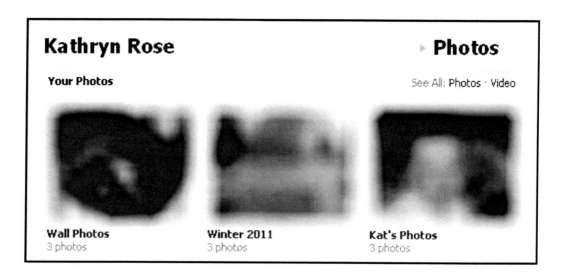

If you already uploaded an album or a photo, click on the name, and then you will see an option to "Edit Album" located on the left site. Click on "Edit Album Info" and be taken to a screen where you can make privacy adjustments (photo below).

You can "customize" privacy settings for each of your photos and/or for entire albums.

You also have the ability to "tag" or label people in a photo. For instance, if a photo features one of your Facebook friends, then you can tag or identify that friend in the photo. This sends a notification to that friend telling them they have been tagged, and provides them with a link to see the photo.

To "tag" someone in a photo, just click on their face. A square will appear framing your friend's face and a box will appear that says "type any name or tag". Start typing a friend's name and Facebook will begin to offer you choices.

When your friends are tagged in your photo, they will receive the notification that they have been tagged in a photo include a link to view the photo. They will have the option to "remove tag" if they don't want to be identified.

To do a quick photo post, go to your status update box and either :

Step 1: put in a status update and then click on either photo or video in the "attach" area. You'll be prompted to upload and it's that easy.

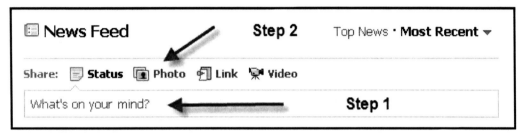

Or just skip to Step 2 and attach a photo with no explanation. It is up to you.

Tagging Photos of People:

As I mentioned in a previous chapter, Facebook offers users the ability to "tag" or label users in a photo. For instance, if a photo contains a user's friend, then the user can tag the friend in the photo. This sends a notification to the friend that they have been tagged, and provides them a link to see the photo.

To "tag" someone in a photo, just click on Tag Photo –

A cross hatch will appear, place it on your friends face and you will see "type any name or tag":

You can begin to type your friend's name, then choose from the list by clicking on the name. You can only tag people if they are your friend.

When your friends are tagged in your photo, they will receive the notification that they have been tagged in a photo including the link to the photo they have been tagged in. They will have the option to "remove tag" if they want to.

Once you are done uploading the pictures, tags and description, at the bottom of the page you'll see a "Save Changes" button. Click that button, go to the top of your page and click "Publish Now" if you're ready. You can also choose to skip that step and not publish right now. Your album will be saved and you can publish it later.

Once you click "publish" your photos go out into your News Feed and are published to your profile. You can view them on your own profile by clicking on the "photos" tab or clicking on the "photos" under your picture:

Sharing Your Photos

You can share this album with your friends even if they are not on Facebook by clicking the "Share This Album" link.

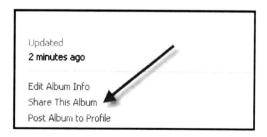

You can now send this to your Facebook friends via private message. You can also share this public link with folks outside of Facebook:

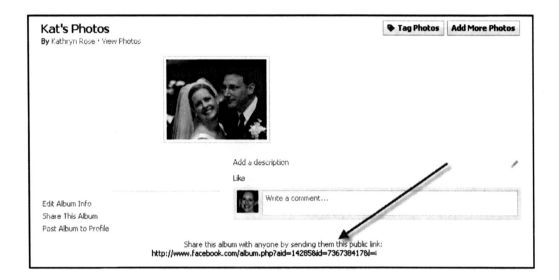

Un-tagging Yourself from Photos/Videos:

People can post photos of you without your permission. You can ask the person to remove a photo that you do not think is flattering but they do not have to if they do not want to. One of the ways to mitigate any potential embarrassment is to "un-tag" yourself from photos. This doesn't remove the photo from Facebook, but if someone doesn't know you by your face, it won't identify you to the world.

Click the "Photo" tab on your main profile page. Select the photo on which you would like to remove the tag

and click "Remove Tag" under the picture. Once you remove the tag, it is removed from the picture, even if the photo appears in your friend's feed.

Chapter 18: Playing Games on Facebook

Many people like to use Facebook to play games. There are thousands of games you can play and enjoy on Facebook. I personally do not play games but I know my teenaged niece and nephew do and so do many others.

This can be a good way to connect with your child. You can access games from the left hand side of your home page.

Once you click on "games," you'll go to a page that lists any games you've already installed, games your friends have played recently, and other games and applications your friends use. At the bottom of this page, you'll see a listing of different types of games you can explore including board games, card games, virtual world games, word games etc.

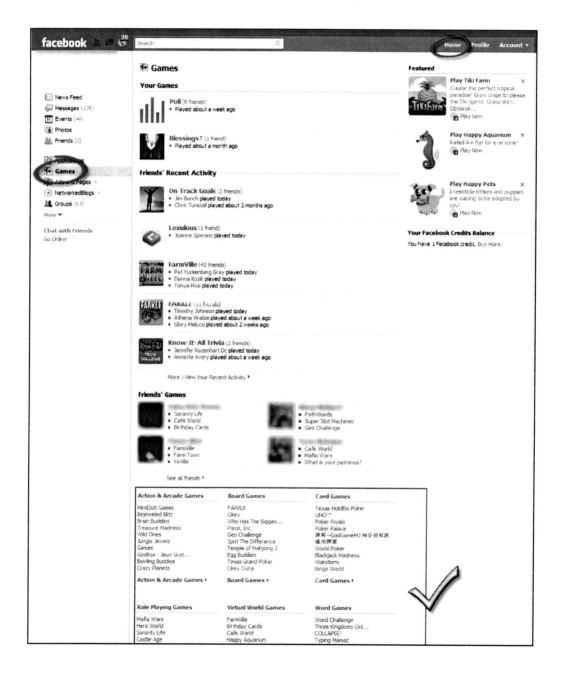

By clicking on any of the categories, you'll be taken to a page where you can choose a game to install. Once you've chosen the application or game, double click on the image and you'll go directly to the application page for that game. Click the "Go to Application" button in blue right under the picture of the game.

Once you click "Go to application" you'll be taken to a page that asks you to "Allow Access." If you want to install this game, click "Allow."

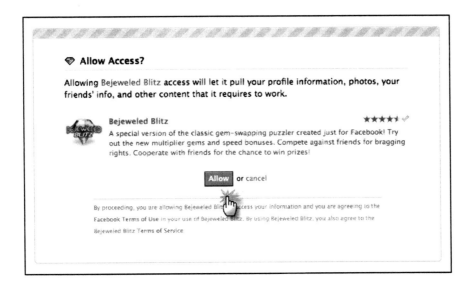

You can always delete any games you decide you don't like. So have fun exploring the games section of Facebook.

Final Words

I hope that I helped you engage online with your children, friends, extended family and colleagues by giving you the inside track to Facebook.

Be sure to have the conversation with your children about their activities on Facebook. It's okay to bring things up that are happening online, because it is just another place where you *all* hang out. I think my responsibility, as a parent, is to teach my child how to be kind, polite, respectful, and have good manners in all social situations so he can become a respected adult. The online communities are just a bit larger and the messages travel faster, so the importance of learning proper and safe usage right from the beginning is heightened.

I expect that you will have a great experience on Facebook and as you use it on a daily basis, you will become more comfortable and most of all have fun with it!

Facebook Usage Contract

I have read a lot about these online usage contracts and I think having a contract between you and your younger teens about their rights and responsibilities when using Facebook can help you set and monitor expectations, start an important conversation between you and your teen and serve as a reminder when rules are ignored. I offer this as a model and invite you to modify or add to it to represent your individual needs.

Family Facebook Users Contract

1. I agree to sit with my parents and go through the privacy settings on my profile and make sure all personal contact information is excluded.
2. I will speak to my parents before accepting someone as a friend.
3. I will ask my parent's permission before uploading any photos to Facebook and then make sure the privacy privileges are set properly.
4. I will take my name off of any Facebook or Search Engine searches
5. I will speak to my parents before downloading any applications on Facebook.
6. My parents will have the username and password to my account and my parents agree not to post anything I deem embarrassing on my wall.
7. I understand that something I post today can be damaging to me in the future so before posting anything I will ask myself "is this something I would want my mother to read?"
8. I will work with my parents to establish online time limits that work for both parties.
9. I will never post anything negative, hurtful or threatening to anyone including family members, teachers or others on Facebook and will tell my parents immediately if I see others doing so.

I understand that any violations of these rules will cause my Facebook privileges to be suspended and may result in my Facebook profile being deactivated.

Signed _____   Dated_____

CPSIA information can be obtained at www.ICGtesting.com
Printed in the USA
LVOW051709190112

264663LV00004B/23/P